Reflect on
I am saying,)
will give you un
in everyt
2 Tim

Salesian Missio
generous poet fri
material include
acknowledgments
notification, will

Cover photo: ©Ph

First Edition Print

The intent and
purpose of this volume is to
give you faith, hope and
inspiration. Hopefully it will help bring
peace and tranquility into your life. May
t be a reminder of God's love, guidance
and His many blessings.

ur publications help to support our work
or needy children in over 120 countries
around the world. Through our
programs, thousands of children are
fed, clothed, educated, sheltered
and given the opportunity to
live decent lives.

s wishes to extend special thanks and gratitude to
nds and to the publishers who have given us permission to re
in this book. Every effort has been made to give p
Any omissions or errors are deeply regretted, and the publisher,
pleased to make the necessary corrections in subsequent editi

y Salesian Missions, 2 Lefevre Lane, New Rochelle, NY 10801-
©53154

todisc/Fotosearch Stock Photography

d in the U.S.A. by Concord Litho Group, Concord, NH 03301.

Reflections of Peace
from the
Salesian Collection

Compiled and Edited
by Jennifer Grimaldi

Illustrated by
Russell Bushée, Terrie Meider,
Bob Pantelone, Frank Massa,
Maureen McCarthy, Paul Scully
and Robert VanSteinburg

Contents

*The Lord is my strength and
my shield, in whom my heart
trusted and found help.
So my heart rejoices; with my
song I praise my God.*
Psalm 28:7

Give Me Strength

Give me strength, oh precious Lord;
Uplift my soul today.
My heart is full of sadness, Lord,
And painful is the way.

Give me strength, oh precious Lord;
Come fill my life with hope.
Bestow on me Thy gentle faith,
And help me, Lord, to cope.

Give me strength, oh precious Lord,
My life I give to Thee.
Hold me, dear Master, in Thy hand,
And set my spirit free!

Hope C. Oberhelman

*My strength and my courage is the
Lord, and He has been my Savior.
He is my God, I praise Him; the God
of my Father, I extol Him.*
Exodus 15:2

To Walk With Christ

To walk with Christ,
To follow His way,
Is to know His love
By night or by day.

To hear His voice
On the mountain peaks,
Or low in the valley
Whenever He speaks...

Is to be aware
Of His presence nearby,
In the sun or the rain,
On the earth, in the sky.

To feel His touch
Through pain and sorrow,
To gather the strength
To face tomorrow.

These are the ways
To live your life,
In times of joy,
In times of strife.

If you walk with Christ,
You will understand
God's place for you
Is the palm of His hand.

Jean Conder Soule

God Will Lead the Way

When the path we walk is lonely
And we feel we need a friend
To walk the straight and narrow,
With its twists and turns and bends…

Then know that our precious Savior
Will be walking by our side,
To talk with us and comfort us
And to be our loving guide.

Sometimes we tend to stumble
On the rocks and pebbles there,
But our Savior will not let us fall
Because He loves us and He cares.

If we always walk the narrow path
And never tend to stray,
Then we know deep within our hearts
That our God will lead the way.

Shirley Hile Powell

Friendships Are Formed

Friendship comes in many forms
And grows as time goes by.
It's never from "coincidence,"
But from a place on high.

It's God who causes paths to cross,
And He who builds the bridge.
It reaches clear across the earth;
No mountain is too big.

Those special friendships we all know
Were seasoned with a plan,
Formed and gathered by His grace,
And safe within God's hand.

Jill Lemming

*For a sun and shield is the Lord God,
bestowing all grace and glory. The
Lord withholds no good thing from
those who walk without reproach.*
Psalm 84:12

You Are There

When I am weary, You are there
To ease my heavy load.
When my path is rocky, You are there
To smooth out every road.

When my heart is aching, You are there
To wipe away my tears.
When I am apprehensive, You are there
To dispel my doubts and fears.

When I am lonely, You are there
To keep me company.
When I feel imprisoned, You are there
To set my locked heart free.

When I am sick, You are there
To make my body well once more.
When I am depressed, You are there
To lift my spirits and make them soar.

When there is anger, You are there
To remove all of the strife.
And when it's time for me to go,
You've promised me Eternal Life.

Savior, tell me now what I must do,
Your goodness to repay.
He answered, "Just believe in Me,
There is no other way."

Elise Alimboyoguen

A Praying Friend

In this world God gives us gifts
To shower us with love.
His blessings all around us
Are sent from up above.

The sunrise in the morning,
The star-filled sky at night –
The seasons, what a wonder,
Fill me with delight.

The blessings of my family,
For food and clothes to wear –
No sweeter gift have I received
Than a praying friend who cares.

Mary Ann Jameson

He's Always There

He's always there to guide us
When we're lost along the way,
When troubles overwhelm us
And we lose the light of day.

He's always there for comfort
When our hearts are filled with pain,
When tears well up inside us
And come down like falling rain.

He's always there to hear us
When we need a listening ear,
When no one understands us
And our hearts are filled with fear.

He's always there to love us
When our burden's hard to bear.
So call Him, He will answer,
And you'll know He's always there.

Vivian Chretien

*O Lord, there is no one like You
and there is no God but You, just
as we have always understood.*
1 Chronicles 17:20

Thank You, God

For every joy and every smile,
Each thing that helps make life worthwhile,
The touch of morning just at dawn,
And twilight hours when day is gone,
For happy, joyful springtime days,
The Summer rain and carefree ways…

For gentle stars that light the night,
A harvest moon all shining bright,
The sound of birdsong in the trees
And fragrant lilacs on the breeze,
A country lane that leads to home
And childhood laughter I have known…

The peace that fills this heart of mine
And every precious hour of time,
The quiet moments I so love,
The magic blue of skies above,
The miracle of upturned sod,
For life so rich, I thank You, God.

Garnett Ann Schultz

Joy and Beauty

Let me always find joy and beauty
In everything that I do or see,
For it shines in all God's glory,
And it's there for you and me.
You can hear it in the laughter
Of the children when they play
Or in the stillness of the evening
As the sky begins to gray.
You can find it in the mountains,
Near the bubbling streams and brooks
Or in the hills and little valleys,
In every corner and every nook.
You can find it in the churches,
And in the big cathedrals, too,
And in the lapping of the ocean,
Or in a garden wet with dew.
But no matter how much beauty
You can find and you can hold –
It will never, ever compare to
A sweet, kind, loving soul!

Sandra Justice

*And be kind to one another,
compassionate, forgiving
one another as God has
forgiven you in Christ.*
Ephesians 4:32

A Pause for Thanks

I pause a moment as the sun
Is rising in the east
To think of things I'm thankful for,
His blessings not the least.

So many wonders come to mind –
The laughter of a child,
A streaking star in midnight skies
Or wintry day turned mild.

Resounding cries of raucous jays,
Perhaps I came too near,
Or of a greening meadow there
Where daffodils appear.

A soaring kite, a billowed sail,
A cup of warming tea;
A clock chimes two in village square,
Though it is really three.

A day of health and happiness,
A night of sweet repose,
A robin's song to herald Spring,
The essence of a rose.

And so my day goes swiftly by;
I cannot name all things
Which give due purpose to my life
And joy that each one brings.

I pause a moment as the sun
Fades slowly in the west;
I count my blessings, thankful that
Each new one seems the best.

Henry W. Gurley

The Power
Of Our Prayers

There comes a time in each one's life
When heartaches will prevail.
Our efforts to control them all
May often falter... fail.
We can cope with daily problems,
Mundane things we might resolve,
Yet overwhelming trials may come
That only God can solve.
When we have faith consistently
And we turn to God in prayer,
He hears and He responds to us,
Embracing us with loving care.
God waits to hear from us each day,
His patience never ceases.
The more we praise and honor Him,
The more His love increases.
When we believe and trust His words,
We form a blessed bond to share,
Transmitted to Almighty God
Through the power of our prayer.

Patience Allison Hartbauer

*My soul shall savor the rich
banquet of praise, with joyous lips
my mouth shall honor You!*
Psalm 63:6

My Treasures

I have a hidden treasure store
That's deep inside my heart.
I tucked away each memory
So it would not depart.

The treasured days of long ago
When childhood cares were few;
Sometimes I gently take them out
And find them fresh and new.

Those barefoot times of long ago,
The magic of each day,
Just knowing Mother was so near
To watch us children play.

The sunlight on the old backyard
Or raindrops on my face,
With children's laughter all around—
Oh, such a happy place!

The fluffy clouds and skies so blue,
Sometimes a gentle rain,
And if the tears should fall, then Mom
Would kiss away the pain.

The years brought many treasures
That I safely tucked away.
The cycle of a life is filled
With treasures every day.

And we should cherish every one,
Each memory in our hearts.
No wealth or fame can e'er replace
Those lovely works of art.

Gertrude B. McClain

The Lord Is With Me

The Lord is with me;
He's always near
To give me strength
And ease my fear.

Though I may struggle
And sometimes I fall,
He loves me completely
In spite of it all.

The Lord is with me;
I bask in His glow.
His glory surrounds me;
His greatness I know.

A. Keeper

Favors From Heaven

On bended knees at the close of the day,
I put my fears and doubts away.
I won't complain and cry and moan;
I'll just give thanks for mercies shown.
I'll thank my Father up above
For all the ways He's shown me love.
The shelter I needed, He did supply,
The sun so warm in a clear blue sky.
Food and water, a featherbed,
A place to rest my weary head.
The clothes I needed, shoes for my feet,
The smell of Spring, flowers so sweet.
Kindness from neighbors, a loaf of bread,
A smile from a child, with sweet words said.
The air I breathe, "sweet breath of life,"
Favors from Heaven, on these I rely.
On bended knees at the close of this day,
I'll give thanks for favors that came my way.

M. I. Cobia

*Above all, give praise to your
Creator, who showers His
favors upon you.*
Sirach 32:13

Let Me Be a Blessing

Forever longing to be free,
To hear Your voice so sweet...
To be a blessing in this world
To others that I meet.

To kiss the face of a crying child
And know it's You I see...
Giving, caring, every day –
Lord, work Your way in me.

To soften someone else's steps,
To know it's not by chance...
That only You prepare the way
And form each circumstance.

Jill Lemming

Giving Thanks

I never cease to marvel
At the wonder of God's world –
Flowers, trees and songbirds,
And tiny leaves unfurled.

I lift my eyes to Heaven,
To skies so soft and blue,
And marvel how each day, our God
Sends His gifts anew.

The gentle rain, the Summer sun,
The harvest in the Fall;
From out the fullness of the earth,
God blesses one and all.

In gratitude I bow my head
And send a prayer above,
Giving thanks for all His gifts
And for His precious love!

Kay Hoffman

*And whatever you do, in word or
in deed, do everything in the name
of the Lord Jesus, giving thanks to
God the Father through Him.*
Colossians 3:17

Look to the Lord

When doubts and fears assail me, Lord,
Help me to look to Thee.
Upon myself I can't rely,
For there's no strength in me.
I need to be reminded, Lord,
I'm here for just a while.
I must do the best I can
And to others bring a smile.
If I have left undone some task
That You would have me do,
Forgive me, Lord, for I know so well
I owe my all to You.
I thank You again today, dear Lord,
As I have so oft before,
For the blessings You have given me,
And I know there's so much more.

May I see naught but the good, dear Lord,
In the friends that I have made
And help them try to understand
The times that I have strayed.
But, oh, the joys that await me
In the wonderful heavenly sphere –
Let me carry my burdens with a smile,
Knowing it's only a short time I'm here,
Then my spirit, like the bird,
Will soar toward the sky
To greet my Lord and my loved ones,
Without another goodbye.

Thelma Grace Ide

My Shepherd
And My Keeper

My God and I walk down life's road
Together, side by side;
On right-of-ways and round the bends,
He is my constant guide.

He leads in paths of righteousness
With blessings overlaid,
For this is what He promises
If we will but obey.

My God and I walk down life's path
Together, day by day;
I keep my eyes upon the Lord
As He shows me the way.

He leads me over obstacles
I could not mount alone;
He is the one who shepherds me –
He's the keeper of my soul.

Loise Pinkerton Fritz

*The Lord is thy keeper: the Lord
is thy shade upon thy right hand.*
Psalm 121:5

Requests

Help me to hear You, Father,
When I close my eyes to pray
And beg for Your direction
As I strive to find my way.

I've made so many choices
In this life You've given me;
So many were the wrong ones,
But I yearn so much to see...

What the best way is to please You,
What the right road is to take,
How to give myself entirely
To a life lived for Your sake.

Forgive me, hold me, help me, Lord
Remind me You are King;
Please take away all doubts from me
And grant me just one thing…

An open heart to take the love
That You so freely give;
And share this heart with everyone
So that I may truly live.

Norma Sullivan

...the birds of Heaven
nest; among the
branches they sing.
Psalm 104:12

I Thank the Lord

I thank the Lord who gave me eyes
To view the clear blue azure skies,
To gaze upon sunflower's gold,
To survey springtime's beauty bold.

I thank the Lord who gave me ears
To hear sweet songbird souvenirs,
To listen to the ocean's roar,
To hear waves pounding on the shore.

I thank the Lord who gave me days
To linger long on life's pathways,
To behold a harvest moonlit night,
To watch a falling star in flight.

I thank Thee, Lord, for these.

Nora M. Bozeman

*Look up to the skies and
behold; regard the heavens
high above you.*
Job 35:5

Give Help

Give help where it is wanted,
Give help to those who need.
It's one of life's great pleasures,
Not just a simple deed.
A smile, a word of friendly praise,
As you pursue your days,
Makes it a little easier
To emulate God's ways.

JoAnne Klikas Studer

Best Gift of All

The best gift of all
Doesn't cost a dime;
Giving someone in need
Some of your time.

A gift can be things you do,
Surprises that you make;
Doing something nice each day
For someone else's sake.

It could be taking a minute
To call a friend who's blue;
In this case your gift is
A friendly, "How are you?"

A gift isn't always a package
Tied up with a bow;
It's remembering with love
Someone that you know.

Ruth Moyer Gilmour

*Beloved, let us love one
another, because love is of God;
everyone who loves is begotten
by God and knows God.*
1 John 4:7

I Tremble With Awe

I tremble with awe when I watch a moon rise,
I marvel at bees as they work in their hive,
And I feel great joy at the mirth of a child
Or watching the animals romp in the wild.
I tremble with awe watching bison in herds,
And I marvel at the migration of birds
And wild geese in flight in the shape of a "V"
Or foliage on an autumnal tree.
I tremble with awe when I see a sunset
With crimson and blues then turning to jet.
I marvel at birds as they nest in the trees;
Peace walks with me in a summertime breeze.
I tremble with awe when I smell the perfume
Of flowers just picked in April or June.
I marvel at hues of the colors they bring
To gratify me in the middle of Spring.
I tremble with awe when a rainbow appears,
Just after a rain and the sun reappears.
I marvel at all our Creator prepared
To bring people delight – I'm so grateful He cared!

Luther Elvis Albright

Everlasting

Life is a blessing
To cherish each day,
To nurture with gladness
In our own special way,
To share with each other
With faith, trust, and love,
Secure in knowing
God guides from above

Vi B. Chevalier

My Prayer for You

May your life be filled with peace
And happiness to spare,
May it be blessed with family
And those for whom you care,
May you enjoy good health and love
Til you are old and gray,
May all your dreams and wishes
Fill your heart each day.
Whatever you may seek in life
I pray that you will find,
And may your life be filled with friends
Who are gentle and kind.
But most of all may you be blessed
With gifts from God above,
May He be at your side each day
And fill your heart with love.

Bill Seebauer

My Prayer

Lord, let me put my hand in Thine –
This is my humble plea.
I cannot find my way alone,
Please, help me walk with Thee.

You know the way that I must go,
You know what's best for me.
I only ask You for Your hand,
Lord, help me walk with Thee.

Sometimes I've stumbled by myself
And fell in deep despair.
Do not let me fall again –
This is my earnest prayer.

I need Your guiding hand,
Dear Lord, I beg on bended knee.
Lord, lift me up and hold my hand
And help me walk with Thee.

Walter John Diehl

The Lord has heard my prayer;
the Lord takes up my plea.
Psalm 6:10

Life

Life is not so lonely
When we share it with a friend,
When we reach out to others
With a helping hand to lend,
When we comfort a broken heart
Or just give a tender smile…
Life is not so lonely
When with others we walk the mile.

Evangeline Carey

He Leads Me

He leads me throughout the day
And answers all of my prayers.
He is my life's salvation –
I know He is always there.
Though toil and turmoil come to me,
I know it is part of life.
With His strength to help guide me,
I can make it through the strife.
My soul cries from hunger
That only He can fill.
Every day I try my very best
To do His holy will.
Our God is kind and merciful,
He lives within you and me,
And never tires of helping us
To be the best that we can be.
My heart is filled with love and joy
Because He leads the way.
I pray to always follow Him
And never chance to stray.

Shirley Hile Powell

The Way...

I looked for hope and did not find it;
I looked for faith and could not pray –
I looked for joy and just felt sadness;
I looked for God and found the way!

Hope C. Oberhelman

Reason to Praise

You give me reason to praise You, Lord,
With every breath I take,
For only You make possible
Every move I make.

Each happy little blessing
That ever comes my way
Is never a coincidence,
But You who lights the way.

And when I'm sad and feel alone
And no one understands,
You're always there when I reach up
To gladly take my hand.

Oh, what comfort and joy to know
I have a Friend so true!
For every time I seek Your will,
You show me what to do.

So hear my praise I offer You,
It's bursting from my heart –
And each new day I walk with You
Just makes more praises start!

Denise A. DeWald

*I will bless the Lord at all
times; Praise shall always
be in my mouth.*
Psalm 34:2

My Faithful Friend

From Heaven God did let descend,
A cherished one, my faithful friend.
An angel without wings, you see,
Who walks life's perilous ways with me.

One in whom I can confide
And when in need is at my side.
She brings sunshine into my day
Through her generous and loving ways.

She tells me I am in her prayers,
I know how genuinely she cares.
I give thanks to my God above
For sending me this gift of love.

Shirley Hile Powell

God Is Always Near

God is ever present.
He's in my life each day.
He holds my hand
And guides my feet
As I walk along the way.

God is like a beacon
As I ride out the storm.
He steers me 'round
The rocks and reefs
And I harbor safe and warm.

God is my good shepherd
And I His humble lamb.
He feeds my soul
In pastures green –
How thankful, Lord, I am.

Gertrude B. Byram

*For you had gone astray like
sheep, but you have now
returned to the Shepherd and
Guardian of your souls.*
1 Peter 2:25

Thank You, Lord

Thank You, Lord, for love and laughter,
All the blessings that You give,
For the love You give so freely
Every day, Lord, that I live…

For the joy You always give me
And the peace so deep within.
Thank You for the strength to conquer
All the fears that are known to men.

Thank You for Your precious word, Lord,
And the gift of prayer so sweet,
Knowing, Lord, You hear each heart cry
From Your heavenly mercy seat.

Lord of Lords, oh King of Glory,
Lamb of God, You died for me.
I could never, ever thank You
For salvation, full and free.

Lord, I cannot help but thank You
For the many things You do.
May I overflow with love, Lord,
Be a blessing, Lord, for You.

Gertrude B. McClain

I Know

When Winter turns to shining Spring
And birds begin to nest and sing,
The world so quickly comes alive
With bursting buds and bees in hive.
The lovely world is all aglow…
'Tis then there is a God, I know.
Who else can change the skies to blue
And bid the sun come shining through,
Can dress the naked trees again
And send a gentle April rain?
So many blessings ours to share
As God then answers heartfelt prayer.
Who else can calm the angry sea,
Can grow a lovely climbing tree,
And color Autumn leaves so bright,
A sunny day – a star-filled night,
A Heaven high – a world below..?
There really is a God, I know.

Garnett Ann Schultz

Garden of Memories

My garden of memories,
Like my garden of flowers,
Brings joys that I treasure
For hours and hours.

Whenever I'm lonely
Or feeling quite blue,
I gather an armful
Of memories of you...

Of days filled with laughter
And sweet childhood play,
Enriched by a friendship
More precious today.

And as I remember
The bond that we share,
My heart brims with gladness
Knowing you, too, still care...

For though the years lengthen
And we're now miles apart,
You'll always bring sunshine
And joy to my heart.

Vi B. Chevalier

*I keep the Lord always before me;
with the Lord at my right, I shall
never be shaken. Therefore my
heart is glad, my soul rejoices; my
body also dwells secure.*
Psalm 16:8,9

There Is a Path

There is a path we each must trod
Upon the road of life
That leads us to our destiny
Of happiness or strife.
Some seek the road less traveled
Or blaze a brand-new trail,
While others seek a common road
Afraid that they will fail.
Some linger at the crossroads,
Unable to decide.
They truly fear the "great unknown"
Because they have no guide.

There is a path we each must choose,
A cross we each must bear,
But no one has to walk alone
Because our God is there!
His word's a light unto our path,
A beacon in the night;
He guides us through the storms of life
And leads us to the light.

Clay Harrison

A True Friend

A friend that lends a helping hand
Is truly a gift from God.
They help to share our burdens
As we walk this earthly sod.
When we are down and feeling low
And our hearts are sad and blue,
Thank God above for faithful friends
Who always help us through.
A friend is like the sunshine
That breaks through clouds of gray.
They're there to ease our heartaches
And to chase our blues away.
Oh yes, they're like a precious jewel.
They are trustworthy and true.
Give thanks to God for sincere friends
And for giving them to you.

Shirley Hile Powell

Toward Fulfillment

What a pleasant place this world would be
If we could but agree
To treat each other always
As we would treated be.

A sunny disposition,
A friendly, ready smile,
A willingness to lend a hand,
To walk the second mile.

Many long for fame and fortune.
On some, power seems to fall,
But the one who serves his brothers
Heeds the noblest call of all.

As this span of days is over,
Fame and fortune fade away,
But the good we do for others
Marks the measure of our days.

Natalie S. Thistle

I have made vows to You, God;
with offerings I will fulfill them.
Psalm 56:13

Friendship

When you plant a seed of friendship,
Nurture it with loving care.
It will blossom with a beauty
That is far beyond compare.

Even when it's in full flower,
As many friendships do,
It still needs food and watering
To keep its bloom like new.

So hold each heartfelt blossom close
That blooms from friendships sown,
And there you'll find them with the rest
Of treasured things you own.

Wilma Barth Roberts

His Loving Care

Jesus watches day by day,
His flowers that bloom along the way,
And all His sheep, grazing there,
He tends each one with loving care.
He gives us sunshine and the rain;
He gives us joy to lessen pain.

Wherever we go, whatever we do,
He gives us each a task to do.
Some may err and some may wan,
But the brave and strong will carry on.
His light shines, tho' the world be dim.
We must leave our plan to follow Him.

O' Jesus, watch with loving care,
Tho' we be scattered everywhere,
And help us each be brave and true,
While trying here to follow You.
We thank You for each blessing given,
But most of all, thank You for Heaven.

Effie Brown

*Listen, my faithful children: open
up your petals, like roses planted
near running waters.*
Sirach 39:13

My Friend

Each evening when the sun goes down
And stars come into view,
Before I close my eyes in sleep
I say a prayer for you.

Of all the blessings I enjoy,
You mean the most to me.
In my thoughts and in my heart,
That's where you'll always be.

We laughed together through the years,
We shared the quiet hours,
And when the skies were wet with rain
You helped me see the flowers.

When my time on earth is through
And life comes to an end,
The gift I'll thank my Maker for
Was making you my friend.

J. Shields

God Stepped
In When I Let Go

O Lord, let me never stray
From Your loving side.
I did so once, not long ago,
And from You tried to hide.

It was easier for me to run
Than face my tears and pain.
I wouldn't lay it at Your feet
And trust Your holy Name.

The world, it offered no relief,
I tried most everything.
My bitterness began to grow,
For I ignored my King.

Then one day I'd had enough,
I gave it all to You.
You helped me through my agony –
I saw what You can do.

You stepped in when I let go,
My peace and healing began.
Though the hill I climb is sometimes steep,
With Your hand in mine, we can.

Denise A. DeWald

You Must Believe

You must believe tomorrow
Will be a better day,
To drive the apprehension
That you possess away.

You must believe with faith in God,
All things on earth can be,
Converted from but wishful thoughts
Into reality.

You must believe the goals you seek
Are never sought in vain,
And with true faith in heart and mind,
Each one you can attain.

Harold F. Mohn

Along Life's Highway

I can see Jesus
In the sunshine of day;
I can hear angels
In the children at play...

I can see Heaven
In the bloom of a flower,
Blessings and splendor
That brighten the hour.

Roses are perfect,
If only a few,
Secluded in gardens
And kissed by the dew.

I can see Jesus
Along life's highway,
In the trees and the mountains
And hills far away.

Katherine Smith Matheney

Praise the Lord from the earth... you mountains and all hills, fruit trees and all cedars.
Psalm 148:7,9

This Alone

My soul and Jesus walked a while
Then settled on the hill.
My heart within beat faster –
Be still, my heart, be still.

My soul and Jesus rested now
Beneath a shady tree;
All the while I wondered
What my God would say to me!

Would there be a slight reproof
For actions I omitted?
Would there be reminders of
Some past sin I committed?

Will He turn two tear-filled eyes
And set their gaze on me?
Oh, say it now, Lord, say it –
No matter what it be!

His sacred lips then parted,
The voice was from above,
Then Jesus spoke one single word,
And that one word was "love."

Sr. Georgeanne Farrell, FSP

Traveling Companions

Traveling companions in life, you see,
Are important along the way;
You need their friendship and advice
As you journey through each day.

Some are only fair-weather friends
Who disappear in storms;
Others stay close by your side,
Their friendship truly warms.

These listen closely to your heart
And help you through rough days.
They laugh with you and gladly share
And by your side they'll stay.

But there's one "Friend" greater than all
Who travels by your side
His name is Jesus Christ, the Lord…
Please, let Him be your Guide!

Charleen Bichel

*Guide me in Your truth and
teach me, for You are God
my Savior. For You I wait all
the long day, because of
Your goodness, Lord.*
Psalm 25:5

Assurance

Although the storms of life abound,
I do not walk alone,
For in God's holy word He says
That He has sent His Son
To be there when the storm clouds come,
When darkness hovers near –
To give a wearied soul its rest,
And drive away its fear.
When worries come with heavy loads,
Alone – I cannot bear;
Through prayer, a lighter load I find,
And know my Savior's there.

Mary S. Chevalier

My Heavenly Companion

I wanted someone to listen,
With an ever-open ear,
I found that special someone,
Who never fails to hear…

I needed someone to guide me
And give my eyes the sight
To follow the road ahead,
And I was given a golden light…

I yearned for someone to catch me
If I should falter and fall,
And right or wrong I found comfort
With someone who'd help me stand tall…

I found the one I needed,
On whom I could always depend;
I had only to look to the heavens,
And choose to make God my friend.

Eleanor Torchia

*Help me, Lord, my
God; save me in
Your kindness.*
Psalm 109:26

Home

They say home is where the heart is,
The place you store your smile,
Where no matter when you travel,
Returning's worth the while...
The place you made your memories,
Where friends and family dwell,
Where someone always listens
When you have tales to tell.

Home is where your peace is,
The place where you are you,
Where there is always something
That you can find to do.
Home has no surprises;
Familiar reigns supreme,
The place you plan your future,
Reminisce, and dream your dreams.

Where strangers don't surround you
And days pass by with speed,
Where your joy is just in being
And you have no greater need.
Home is where your soul lives,
Where your past is all around,
Where the sunshine is the brightest.
Home… no sweeter sound!

Sharon Franco

As the sparrow finds a home and the
swallow a nest to settle her young.
My home is by Your altars, Lord of
hosts, my King and my God!
Psalm 84:4

Not My Will,
But Thine, Father

He awakened from His sleep
Before the break of day
To find a place of solitude
Where He could kneel and pray.
His spirit, quiet and gentle,
Was as a little lamb.
His soul, bold as a lion;
His body, that of man.
In prayer, He sought His Father
Before the rising sun,
That He might work His perfect will
Before the day was done.

Eva Marie Stover

He's Always There

When I awake each morning
About to start my day,
I thank the Father, high above,
And then I'm on my way.

And when the day is over,
I quiet down and pray,
And thank Him for the gifts He gives
And help along the way.

He's always there to guide me.
He never leaves my side.
He always shows His love for me.
In Him I can confide.

I never have to feel afraid
When God is in my heart.
His love will chase all fears away
And make all pain depart.

Sheila B. Roark

Teach me to do Your will, for
You are my God. May Your
kind spirit guide me on
ground that is level.
Psalm 143:10

My Daily Prayer

Give me a spirit sweet, Lord,
As I go about my day,
That I would be a blessing
To someone on life's way.

Let no pettiness of mine
Keep me from doing good,
To help where there's a need,
Love my neighbor as I should.

When I would seek my will, not Yours,
Speak to my heart anew;
Give me a vision clear, dear Lord,
Of what You'd have me do.

Grant to me the courage
To stand up for right and good,
Rememb'ring that we all should live
In a kindly brotherhood.

Let me not be boastful
About some good I may have done;
Keep me ever mindful
That from You my blessings come.

I do not ask for riches
Nor skies forever fair,
A closer walk with You, dear Lord –
This is my daily prayer.

Kay Hoffman

Prayer

If you can pray for others
When your heart suffers, too...
If you can ease another's pain
By any act you do –
If you can laugh when others
Would only pause to weep...
If you can gather courage
When the road is growing steep –
Then God will not forget you
For everything you do.
The more you give to others,
The more comes back to you.

Florence Powers

A Blessing Right Next Door

There's nothing like a neighbor,
Who's kind, and dear, and warm,
To talk with over coffee,
And make you feel at home.

If you want to kick your shoes off,
They wouldn't mind at all.
And if I ever needed help,
It's on them I would call.

Their hearts are full of compassion,
If I should shed a tear.
They'd hold my hand so tenderly
To let me know they care.

Oh, thank You, God, for neighbors,
Your blessings right next door.
This special gift of friendship,
I could not ask for more.

Mary Ann Jameson

When you hearken to the voice of the Lord, your God, all these blessings will come upon you and overwhelm you.
Deuteronomy 28:2

Search Every Heart

Search the heart of every man;
Try to see and understand.
See the pain that can't be told,
The hope, the fear, in every soul.
Offer love, do not condemn;
What you give comes back again!
Good or bad can both be sown,
Search every heart – first your own!

Rose M. Schrantz

Dear Lord and Master

Dear Lord and Master of my life,
I give my heart to Thee.
I need Thee, everlasting Lord,
To set my spirit free.

Dear Lord and Master of my life,
Renew my waning will.
My heart and soul are Thine, oh Lord,
And I adore Thee still.

Dear Lord and Master of my life,
Please take away my cares.
I love Thee, oh my blessed Lord…
Come listen to my prayers.

Hope C. Oberhelman

Heaven Is My Home

I know that Heaven is my home –
In subtle little ways,
I feel its pull upon my life
Throughout the passing days.
At times there washes over me
The feeling I have been
Lifted by a tidal wave
And then set down again.
I'm very well aware that I
Am only "passing through"
This world, and so I try to do
The best that I can do.
But I know Heaven is my home
Since very long ago.
I've always felt it in my heart;
Nobody told me so.

But I'm not nearly good enough,
The way I am today.
I need to let God take control
And wash my faults away.
The faded clothes that cover me
Are patched with pride and greed.
I know I've got a way to go
To get the things I need,
But God can see what man cannot,
And His ways are His own,
And I am precious in His sight
And nevermore alone.
And He walks close beside me,
As evening shadows fall,
And with His arms about me,
I am not afraid at all.

Grace E. Easley

My Father's Care

Do you ever walk by a rushing stream
And wonder what song it's singing?
Or stop outside a country church
To listen to the bells ringing?

Don't you love to hear the sounds of night
While sitting on your porch,
And see the splendor of the northern sky
When it lights up like a torch?

And how about mornings after the storm
When there's a cleanness in the air?
These many things all say to me,
"I'm in my Father's care."

Elaine Fowser

Thank You, Lord

Lord, I want to thank You
For the blessings sent my way,
For family and friends who share
Their love and joy each day.

I thank You for my Christian faith
That You generously gave to me,
And for Your help through every trial
And for health and prosperity.

I thank You for the seasons –
Spring, Summer, Winter, and Fall.
My heart is filled with gratitude
For the wonder of it all.

I thank You for Mother Earth
And her beauty, so abundant and rare.
Oh Lord, it would take me a lifetime
To thank You for what You share.

Shirley Hile Powell

*If you and your children are well and your
affairs are going as you wish, I thank God
very much, for my hopes are in heaven.*
2 Maccabees 9:20

A Way of Seeing

On earth we only see, at best,
The closest plans we make,
The nearest moment that we're in,
The smallest steps we take.

Yet high upon a mountaintop,
Surveying all the sky,
I watch a cloud's capricious form
And tiny birds that fly.

While down below the rivulets
Divide the new plowed course;
The little streams gain vigor
And become a treacherous force.

It's then I understand how God
Can look at us and know
What went before, what lies ahead,
For every child below.

And though it's troublesome for us
To face an unknown end,
Thank God, He's in control of life,
Our Guardian and our Friend.

Elizabeth Rosian

God will not allow your foot to slip;
your Guardian does not sleep.
Psalm 121:3

My Dearest Friend

I talk to Him in the morning
When the day is at its best;
I talk to Him at noontime
When my heart is full and blest;
I talk to Him in the evening
When the day is almost complete;
I talk to Him at midnight
When everyone else is asleep.
If I could not talk to my Savior,
To whom else would I go?
He is closer than any other –
He's the dearest Friend I know.

Helen Ruth Ashton

God's Promise

Whenever your heart is hurting,
And you're filled with much despair,
Wherever you turn, friend, for solace,
Remember that God's always there.
Whatever fate brings without warning,
Whatever the trials that you bear,
God's love and His grace will enfold you,
If you turn to Him in prayer.
For He is the rainbow above us,
Awesome for all to see,
Reflecting His promise and glory
When we seek Him implicitly.

Vi B. Chevalier

*God's way is unerring; the
Lord's promise is tried and
true; He is a shield for all
who trust in Him.*
Psalm 18:31

Something to Give...

We all have something we can give
To bless someone where'er we live.
It may be a kindly word or deed
That helps someone in time of need.
To visit someone very dear
Or just a little note of cheer
Will help to chase the gloom away
From another's weary day.
A blessing sweet that we can give,
To be more willing to forgive.
A cup of tea shared with a friend
Can help a broken friendship mend.
A handclasp warm or friendly smile,
A gift that's never out of style...
These little ways that show we care
Are blessings needed everywhere.

Kay Hoffman

*Above all, give praise to your Creator,
who showers His favors upon you.*
Sirach 32:13

God's Springtime
Has Blossomed

Welcome the glorious springtide,
Open the door to the sun;
Let in the scent of this season,
Now that Spring has begun.

Hum with the soft, gentle breezes,
Sing with the birds that now sing;
This is a time of rejoicing,
This is the season of Spring.

Let in the radiant springtide,
Listen to the sounds, see the sights.
Hear all the peepers a-peeping,
See geese in the sky in flight.

Witness rebirth of the flowers,
Discover new life everywhere;
Rejoice! God's springtime has blossomed
Where once all was bleak and bare.

Loise Pinkerton Fritz

*Our days are like the
grass; like flowers of the
field we blossom.*
Psalm 103:15

I Thank You
With a Prayer

My twilight years of rich content
Are filled with love for You.
I seem to feel Your presence, Lord,
In everything that I do.

How bittersweet the yesteryears
When memories start to flow
Of youthful times now past
In those years of long ago.

With age I seem to lose desire
To live life's fast, swift pace.
Now I long to be close to You
And to feel Your sweet embrace.

I'm content to sit and talk with You
Off and on throughout the day
And how I long to walk with You
As I go along life's way.

Earth's beauty that I savor each day
Is a gift beyond compare
And in these times of golden years
I thank You with a prayer.

Shirley Hile Powell

*Learn to savor how good the
Lord is; happy are those who
take refuge in Him.*
Psalm 34:9

He Is There

Have you ever felt the need of a friend
In whom you could confide?
Have you felt the pain of loneliness
Bottled up inside?
Did you know that there is someone
Who will listen when you talk
And lend a sympathetic ear
And lead you where you walk?
He will take your hand in His
And lead you on the way,
He will never fail you!
He is with you every day.
So remember, if you're lonely,
Jesus will be there,
If you open the door to your heart
By whispering a prayer.

Dorothy Schreiner

Life Is Like a Marathon

Life is like a marathon;
A timed and measured race,
And those who best shall run its course
Show discipline and grace…

Life is like a marathon;
One starts as a beginner,
And then must strive for excellence
To finish as a winner…

Life is like a marathon;
With the Savior by your side,
And the wind strong against your back,
God's will shall be your guide!

Hope C. Oberhelman

*You are my rock and my
fortress; for Your name's
sake lead and guide me.*
Psalm 31:4

The Gift of Happiness

If you look to be happy
Then happy you'll be,
For the blues will not stay
When your heart's fancy-free.

Though you may be weary
And your cares multiply,
Just smile and be cheerful
And out the window they'll fly.

If you count all your blessings,
I'm sure you will find
The good far outweighs the bad,
So leave the bad behind.

If you look to be happy,
You'll never be blue,
For God's special gift
Will be given to you.

Nora M. Bozeman

I See God

I see God in the faces of children
Who are smiling with innocent love...
The magnificent light of His glory
Reigns down from the heavens above.

I see God in the joy of my friendships
And I weep at the kindness they've shown...
Reflections of Christ all around me,
I know I am never alone.

I see God in the touch of creation
When the blossoms of springtime arrive...
The season of hope and the promise
That Jesus, my Lord, is alive!

Jill Lemming

*Rise up in splendor! Your
light has come, the glory of
the Lord shines upon you.*
Isaiah 60:1

Time to Step Out

Dear Lord, now the waters
Are dark in my life.
They are troubled with heartache
And stormy with strife.
And here in my boat
I am battered about,
Nearly capsized with fear
And tormented with doubt.
Yet I know with one word
Of Your spoken will,
The seas would be calm,
The waves would be still.
But would I see Your power,
Would I know Your might,
If my faith in You never
Stood test to a fight?
So here in my boat, Lord,
I'm ready to stand.
If You bid me to come, Master,
Stretch forth Your hand.

I'll step from this boat
Onto my troubled sea,
Knowing only that You, Lord,
Are walking with me.
I'll see You then, Jesus,
And know Your great peace.
And it will not matter
Though strivings don't cease.
I'll hold to the hand
That eternally saves.
Lord, we'll stroll on the waters
And dance on the waves!

Robin Gray

There's Beauty in Everything

I'm filled with awesome wonder
At everything I see –
Sweet flowers in my garden,
A golden Autumn tree…
The bird's song in the morning,
The sun high o'er the hill,
The water wheel that's turning
Down by the old grist mill…
The children's shouts of laughter
Out in the woods beyond,
To see the ducks all swimming
Down in the old mill pond…
The bright blue sky above me,
White clouds all drifting by…
I can't quite comprehend it,
And yet so blest am I.
My world is filled with beauty,
My heart is filled with love,
So now I pause to praise Him
And lift my hands above.
There's beauty in everything,
In big things and in small,
So I must thank the Maker
For He hath made them all.

Mary E. Herrington

If My Lord Should Call

If my Lord should call tomorrow,
What would I do today?
Would I leave some heart in sorrow
Because I forgot to pray?
The letters left unwritten,
The words of cheer to spread,
Would I go to meet my Maker
Leaving these things unsaid?
A friend whose heart is broken,
And feeling much despair,
Would I leave until the morrow
Kind words of hope to share?

Could I spend the live-long day
Thinking just of me,
Or try to help another
The words of life to see?
Could I sit in contemplation
While the time draws nigh
Without the words of Jesus
Forever as my guide?
If my Lord should call tomorrow,
Would He a stranger be?
Or could I say "I've waited long
My dearest friend to see."

Dorothy Schreiner

Meditation

The world is silent, white and still;
Deep snow has covered every hill.
The trees stand quiet, almost lost –
Covered with a velvet frost.
The only sounds in Winter air
Are moving branches, dark and bare.
Then in the distance, one lone deer
Runs the fields without a fear.
And as I watch his agile form,
For just a time there is no storm.
And in my memory there is sun
With Summer green and Winter done.

Joan Stephen

Look to Jesus

Look to Jesus when the sun shines,
Feel His presence ever near,
In thy soul know He is sovereign,
Hear His voice speak soft and clear,
"All is well and in your favor,
Lo, with you I am always."
Ponder this, build your faith stronger…
Trust God in this perfect day.
Surely skies will cloud and darken,
Sorrow, too, will fill your soul,
Disappointment may deter you
From your dearest dream and goal.
Hold His hand, for happy moments
Build your faith, affirming trust,
And His nearness will sustain you
When your plans dissolve in dust.
Cling to Jesus, count your blessings;
Then when anguish and despair
Shatter hope and leave you stranded,
You will find Him with you there.

Anna Lee Edwards McAlpin

*The Lord look upon
you kindly and
give you peace!*
Numbers 6:26

Direct All Our Ways

Lord of Everlasting Light,
Draw us closer to You,
Help us to be considerate,
Giving comfort where it's due,
To be understanding
Rather than to be understood,
To daily persevere
For our own good.
Give us enough strength
To face each day,
Guide us through life,
Direct all our ways.
And when despondent,
Leave all in Your care,
Fill us with hope,
Keep us from despair,
Fill us with peace,
Let it gently descend,
To walk in Your light…
Keep us faithful to the end.

Jacqui Richardson

He Is There

No matter the deed, He is in it,
Whatever our need, He is there.
Whether it is trouble or sorrow,
You will find Him faithful, He cares.

In the heat of the battle, He is present,
In the long, lonely nights, in our prayers.
In our suffering and pain, He's there with us.
He knows every need, and He cares.

When we carry God's word in our hearts,
Wherever we go, He'll be there.
He never need fear we'll be lost,
For His presence dwells everywhere.

Theo Cusato

Reaching Out for God

Flying on the wings of faith
Through ever present woes,
Gliding over rocky shores
Where constant troubles flow,
Floating high above the storms,
Driven by each new sorrow,
Longing for a better day,
Hopes and dreams for tomorrow.
Flying on the wings of faith
As through this life I trod.
My prayers drift steadily higher,
Reaching out for God.

Rebecca Sweeney

The Mountain

What is the mountain you stand facing today?
Will you be able to climb to the top?
Or is the way obscured by distractions of life
And the decision to try come to a stop?

Everyone faces insurmountable tasks
From the valley of dark despair,
But the way up and out requires a faith
That God those burdens will bear.

Just take His hand – don't try it alone;
His footsteps are steady and sure.
The worry of failure on the next step up,
You no longer need ever endure.

Don't give up, whatever the struggle;
There's a glorious summit to view.
Experience the triumph when the battle is won;
In the steps of the Savior is glory for you.

Elaine Fowser

God Gives Us Friends

God sends people on our path
Who knows just how we feel…
Kindred spirits from the start,
Soul mates, who are real.
People who have walked our road
And sung our own sweet song…
Friends who give us what we need
And tell us we belong.
Their actions show how much they care
Their words are pure and kind…
Friends who see the best in me,
And I'm so glad you're mine.

Jill Lemming

Arms of Mercy

When trials are your portion
And your night is ever long,
When heartbreak steals your laughter
And your soul has lost its song...
When little comforts leave you
And you're left with stinging tears,
When loneliness envelops
And you're bound by doubt and fears...
Cry out for tender mercies,
Let the Lord's sweet love embrace;
Cast that heavy load upon Him
And look full into His face.
Rest your eyes and heart upon Him,
Let Him ease your every care.
Let Him wipe your tears and sorrow
As you linger with Him there.
Nestling in God's arms of mercy
Brings assurance, hope and peace.
You can know that in your struggles,
God's embrace brings sweet release.

D. Sue Horton

Hear my voice, Lord,
when I call; have mercy
on me and answer me.
Psalm 27:7

The Bridge of Life

In dreams I saw the bridge of life
O'er which each soul must go,
And down beneath the rapids roar
In wildest winds that blow.

The bridge itself is weak and worn
From those that passed before,
With any step the stumbling soul
Might slip and be no more.

And why, thought I, would God so kind
Not mend this dismal way?
Why would He let each precious life
Cross on that bridge each day?

But when I raised my eyes above,
There coming through the night,
I saw an angel, bright with grace,
That shone with love and light.

He stopped beside the ancient bridge
And to this day he stands
Beside each soul that walks thereon
To guide with tender hands.

And then I knew there was no man
Who walked that bridge alone,
For God's own angels guard our way
And light the dark unknown!

Kate Watkins Furman

Thanksgiving

Thank You, Lord, for the Summer days,
The beauty of flowers, warmth of sun,
And for the last pale blossoms
That stayed till the season was done.
Thank You for the Autumn days,
Of sapphire skies, trees on parade
In brilliant colors that I know,
The Master Artist has made.
Thank You for helping me cope
With the trials that came my way,
Thank You for this passing year...
For every hour, for every day.

Virginia Luers

The Joys of Today

I don't live in the past with its many regrets
Nor dwell in the days yet to be.
Today is the day I can face with great joy;
I'm forgiven, a soul set free.

Giving thanks to God for eyes to behold
The beauty of this new dawn,
For ears to hear the cheerful tunes
Of birds, awakening the morn.

For hands to handle, to work and play;
To reach out and touch someone dear.
For arms to shelter and embrace
When heartaches and sorrow draw near.

For feet to walk the extra mile,
Bringing hope to a heart in despair.
For lips to speak a comforting word,
And a smile that says I care.

Regina Wiencek

*A cheerful glance brings joy
to the heart; good news
invigorates the bones.*
Proverbs 15:30

A Prayer of Thanksgiving

For Summer sun and Autumn gold,
For springtime rain and Winter's cold,
For dawn so fair and stars at night,
For darkness that brings morning's light...
Dear God, we thank Thee for the hope
That prayers to You so oft evoke,
For peace that lives within our heart
Because You are so much a part...
For hands that share and hearts that sing
And all the blessings life can bring,
For little feet and childish prayers
That wipe away the worldly cares...

Dear God, we thank Thee on this day
As silently we pause to pray,
We ask Your guidance through the year
To help us banish hate and fear.
For love and faith and friendships true,
For hands to work and work to do,
Tomorrow's dreams that we have planned,
The beauties of this wondrous land,
For life so rich, for untold joys,
The smiles of little girls and boys,
For such a very goodly part...
Dear God, our thanks with all our heart.

Garnett Ann Schultz

Indeed, the grace of our Lord has been
abundant, along with the faith and
love that are in Christ Jesus.
1 Timothy 1:14

Be Thankful

Don't ever forget to be thankful
For every blessing you find on your way;
Each small happiness is a measure
That weighs in for you day after day.

Hold onto the blessings you gather,
Fill your mind with the joy that they give,
Your whole life will take on new meaning,
Build on love and you truly will live.

Lola Neff Merritt

My Secret Place

Within my heart is a secret place
Where safely tucked away
Are all the lovely memories
Of all my yesterdays.

And when of life I'm weary,
I close my eyes and then –
I take those precious memories out
And live them o'er again.

In memories I'm forever young,
Set free from cares and strife,
My heart is light – my feet have wings –
I'm filled with the joy of life!

I cherish all those dream-filled days
That time can ne'er erase,
And so I'll keep them tightly locked
In my secret hiding place.

Marilyn Oakvik

Fear not, beloved, you are safe;
take courage and be strong.
Daniel 10:19

Celebrate Time

Time travels on,
Quickly it mounts.
How we spend time
Is really what counts.

It's just like a train
On a fast track,
Traveling onward –
No turning back!

Celebrate time,
The hour, the day.
Trust in the Lord –
He'll lead the way!

Let your light shine,
Turn away from all sin.
Focus on Jesus –
Let a new day begin!

Yesterday vanished…
Today is now here.
Now is the time,
Have no doubt or fear.

Rejoice and be glad.
Sing a new song.
Celebrate time!
To Him you belong!

Edna Massimilla

Help Us Find True Peace

Sometimes we feel so all alone
As evening shadows fall.
There are so many heartaches,
We're frightened of it all.
The world can be so dark and cold,
It brings us hurt and pain.
We're looking for some sunshine
And all we see is rain.
But if we listen carefully,
God's voice is always near.
He wants to help us smile again
And conquer all our fear.
He comforts when we turn to Him,
He wants our tears to cease.
He wants to walk beside us
And help us find true peace.

Karen Peters

Now

Don't come to pay me homage
Or spill tears upon my stone.
Come now and let me touch you,
Let me know I'm not alone.
I need the sweet assurance
Of your warm and gentle smile.
I yearn to hear your laughter,
Sit beside me for awhile.
When Jesus comes to take me
To my home in Heaven's place,
I'll go in peace, contented
That I've seen your smiling face.
I will not smell the flowers
Or hear you sing my praise.
Bring them now to warm my heart
Throughout my living days.
Your kindness and compassion,
Greater love you can't endow.
Come share these precious moments
While I live… come do it now.

Patience Allison Hartbauer

*Lord, do not withhold
Your compassion from me;
may Your enduring kindness
ever preserve me.*
Psalm 40:12

God's Love

No one living on the earth
Can mend a broken heart.
No one has the power to stop
The teardrops when they start.

Not even our closest friend
Can feel our inner pain,
Or touch our grieving spirit
To make it smile again.

But looking down from up above,
There's One who shares it all,
Who feels our every heartache
And knows when teardrops fall.

And God, in love, wants very much
To give us sweet relief…
To take away our trials,
Our worries and our grief.

Though He longs so greatly
Our hearts and souls to lift,
There are so very many
Who still refuse His gift.

They turn their eyes toward riches
And other earthly gain,
Never understanding why
It does not ease their pain.

And God in sorrow watches;
There's no more He can do.
Isn't it time we opened our hearts
And let His love come through?

Joan Fennell Carringer

Rejoice!

Rejoice! Give thanks to God above
For all good things, and for His love.
In time of need, He's ever near.
His still, small voice our souls can hear.
When sorrow, pain or fear we face,
He sends His peace to take its place.
We can depend upon His word
And know our prayers are always heard.
All things in life He will provide,
As we walk with Him, side by side.
With perfect joy our hearts are blest,
For in His presence, we can rest.
Rejoice! Give thanks to God above,
For all good things, and for His love.

G. Lillian Lewis

Always Carry
An Extra Smile

A smile can be a golden gift
To a sad and lonely heart,
And can't be overrated
As a valued work of art.

A heart gets worn and tattered
From use down through the years,
And may just need a smile or two
To wipe away its tears.

Whether a heart is broken
Or just plain feeling blue,
A little touch of tenderness
Can make the sun shine through.

Catherine Janssen Irwin

*For I long to see you, that I may
share with you some spiritual gift
so that you may be strengthened.*
Romans 1:11

Somewhere Among
The Heartaches

Somewhere among the heartaches,
A blessing may be found
That will somehow make you stronger
And turn your life around.

Somewhere among life's failures
Is the key to a success
That may unlock the future
And lead to happiness.

Somewhere among the doubts and fears
Is a mustard seed of faith
That will somehow dry your tears
And keep you in the race.

Somewhere among life's detours
Is a straight and narrow way
That leads us safely home again
To fight another day.

Somewhere beneath the ice and snow,
The bulbs of Spring abound…
Somewhere among the heartaches
A blessing may be found!

Clay Harrison